HRJC

D1271224

DANGEROUS MAZES

William Potter
Leo Trinidad

WINDMILL BOOKS

Published in 2019 by Windmill Books,
an Imprint of Rosen Publishing
29 East 21st Street, New York, NY 10010

Written by: William Potter
Illustrated by: Leo Trinidad
Designed by: Stefan Holliland with Emma Randall
Edited by: Joe Harris with Julia Adams

Cataloging-in-Publication Data

Names: Potter, William. | Trinidad, Leo, illustrator.
Title: Dangerous mazes / William Potter; illustrated by Leo Trinidad.
Description: New York : Windmill Books, 2019. | Series: Ultimate finger trace mazes | Includes glossary and index.
Identifiers: ISBN 9781538390030 (pbk.) | ISBN 9781508197256 (library bound) | ISBN 9781538390047 (6 pack)
Subjects: LCSH: Maze puzzles--Juvenile literature.
Classification: LCC GV1507.M3 T756 2019 | DDC 793.73'8--dc23

Manufactured in the United States of America

CPSIA Compliance Information: Batch BW19WM: For Further Information contact Rosen Publishing, New York, New York at 1-800-237-9932

CONTENTS

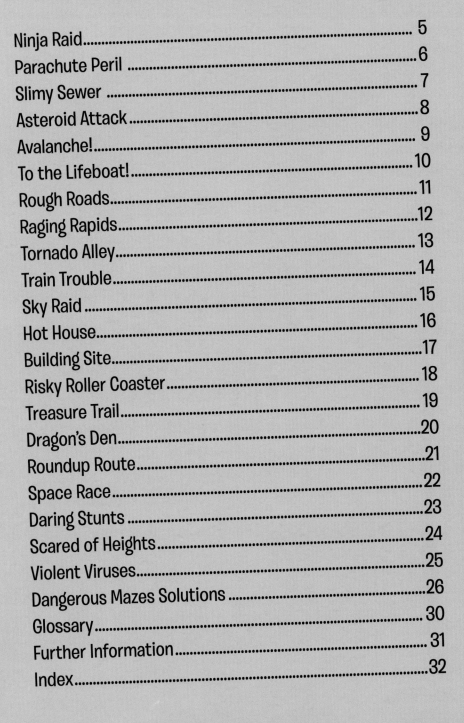

HOW TO USE THIS BOOK

This book is full of high-risk mazes, where you have to help the heroes find a safe path to complete their daring missions. Look out! Every page is packed with perils.

1. READ THE INSTRUCTIONS CAREFULLY BEFORE USING YOUR FINGER TO GUIDE THE HEROES FROM THE START TO THE FINISH.

2. AVOID ALL THE DANGERS. MAKE SURE THE HEROES AREN'T TRAPPED, ZAPPED, OR SNAPPED UP FOR LUNCH!

HELP!

START HERE!

3. OFTEN, SOMEONE NEEDS RESCUING. LEAD THE HEROES THERE FIRST, BEFORE HELPING THEM TO ESCAPE!

4. YOU CAN FIND THE SOLUTIONS TO ALL THE MAZES FROM PAGES 26 TO 29.

NINJA RAID

Help the ninja sneak past the samurai guards and get out the door without being seen.

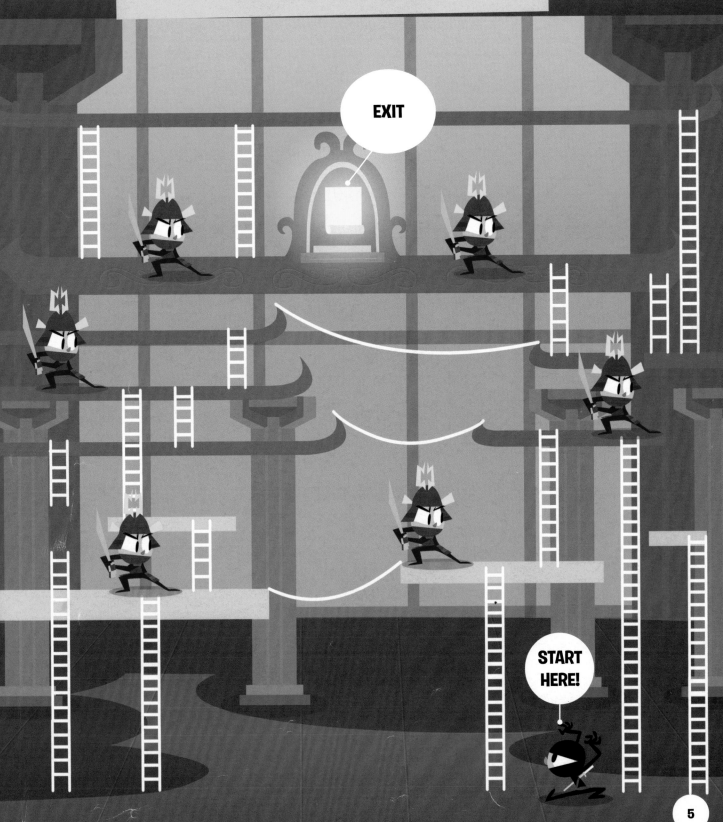

PARACHUTE PERIL

Guide this parachutist to a safe landing, avoiding biting birds, lethal lightning, and a forest of thorns on the ground.

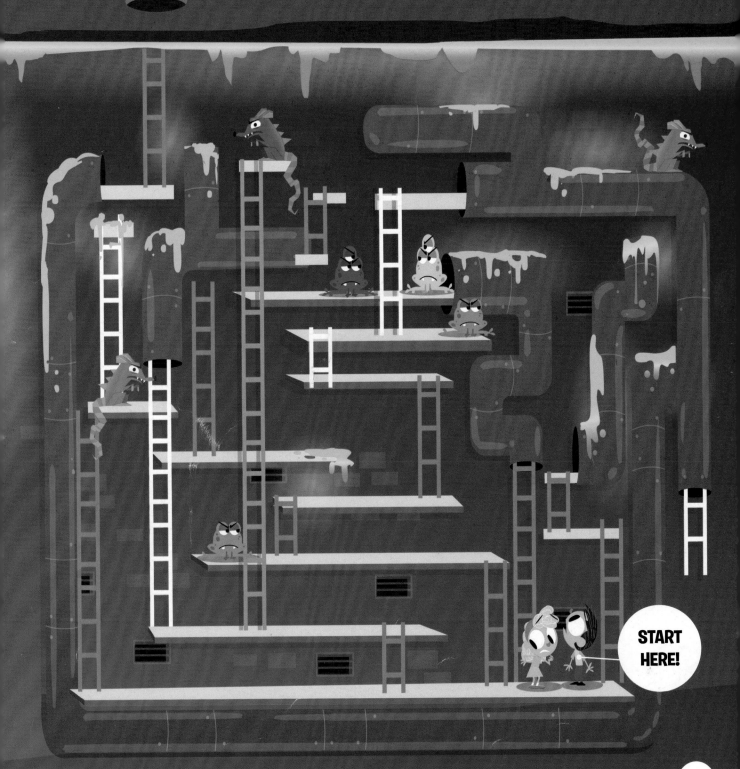

SLIMY SEWER

Radioactive sludge has filled the sewers with moody mutants.
Find a way past the monsters to the sludge-free surface!

SEWER EXIT

START HERE!

ASTEROID ATTACK

Help the astronauts through the asteroid belt to rescue their robot and bring him back to their space shuttle.

START HERE!

AVALANCHE!

Help the skier race away from the avalanche to the rescue plane, without being clawed by grouchy grizzlies.

RESCUE PLANE

RAGING RAPIDS

There's a rough ride over rapids ahead. Lead the boat to safety by dodging the anacondas and piranhas.

START HERE!

SAFE WATERS

TORNADO ALLEY

Caught between terrible twisters, our heroes need to hurry to the safety of an underground bunker without being hit by flying furnishings.

START

SAFETY BUNKER

TRAIN TROUBLE

There's big trouble on the tracks! Direct the engine driver around the obstacles to the exit.

START HERE!

ESCAPE

SKY RAID

Superspies have stolen the enemy's plans. Now, they need to reach their plane and get away from the bad guys' sky base.

START

GETAWAY PLANE

HOT HOUSE

The building's on fire! Find a way for the daring firefighter to reach the girl at the top and return to safety without touching the flames.

HELP!

START HERE!

BUILDING SITE

Underground explorers have ended up below a building site. Hurry them through the tunnels before the path is filled with concrete.

ESCAPE

START HERE!

RISKY ROLLER COASTER

This amusement park ride needs a safety check! With cars left behind, the kids on the roller coaster must find a route over the track to the finish line.

START HERE!

RIDE ENDS

TREASURE TRAIL

Help our heroine reach the buried treasure, avoiding the coconuts, fallen tree, and pillaging pirates!

START

PIRATE
TREASURE

ROUNDUP ROUTE

This young cowboy needs to lasso his first horse. Help him reach the stallion, avoiding the obstacles along the way.

START HERE!

LASSO THE WILD STALLION

SPACE RACE

Lead the rebel pilot to the target to blast the enemy space station's power source.

START HERE!

BLAST THIS!

DARING STUNTS

This skateboarding star is ready for a super stunt. Lead her down the ramps and along the rails, dodging boards and the last guy who tried it!

START HERE!

REACH THE FLAG!

SCARED OF HEIGHTS

This kid is terrified that he'll fall. Climb up to fetch him, but watch out for grumpy gulls.

HELP!

START HERE!

24

VIOLENT VIRUSES

Shrunk in their micro-car, our heroes are now surrounded by viruses. Find a path past them to the growth ray.

START HERE!

GROWTH RAY

DANGEROUS MAZES
SOLUTIONS

PAGE 5

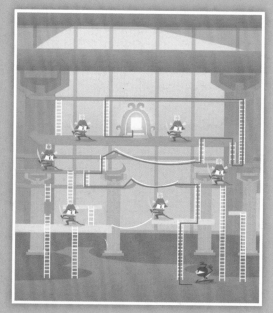

PAGE 6

PAGE 7

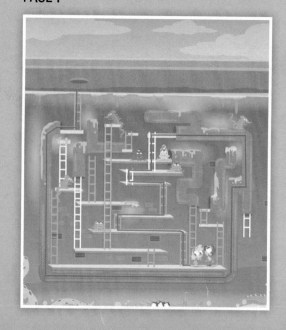

PAGE 8

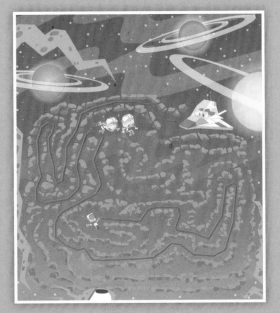

PAGE 9

PAGE 10

PAGE 11

PAGE 12

PAGE 13

PAGE 14

PAGE 15

PAGE 16

PAGE 17

PAGE 18

PAGE 19

PAGE 20

PAGE 21

PAGE 22

PAGE 23

PAGE 24

PAGE 25

GLOSSARY

asteroid belt A ring of asteroids that orbits the sun between Mars and Jupiter.

avalanche A mass of snow, ice, and rocks that rushes down a mountainside very suddenly.

bunker An underground shelter.

lair The home of a wild animal.

lethal Deadly.

mutant A creature that is different from its parents due to changes in its genes.

pillage To steal using force or violence.

radioactive Emitting energy waves that can harm wildlife and humans.

raid A surprise attack on an enemy.

rapids Fast-flowing, often dangerous, parts of a river.

samurai A Japanese warrior.

sewer An underground pipe or tunnel that carries away waste.

stallion A male adult horse that can breed.

tornado A destructive, high-speed, whirling wind that forms a funnel and travels across landscapes.

FURTHER INFORMATION

Books:

Guignard, Theo. *Labyrinth: Find Your Way Through 14 Magical Mazes.* London, UK: Wide Eyed Editions, 2017.

Kamigaki, Hiro. *Pierre the Maze Detective: The Mystery of the Empire Maze Tower.* London, UK: Laurence King Publishing, 2017.

Robson, Kirsteen. *Big Maze Book.* London, UK: Usborne Publishing, 2013.

Smith, Sam. *Around the World Mazes.* London, UK: Usborne Publishing, 2017.

Websites:

For web resources related to the subject of this book, go to: www.windmillbooks.com/weblinks and select this book's title.

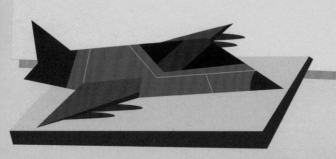

INDEX